What I Want

Also by Kathleen Fraser (limited editions):

WHAT I WANT

Kathleen Fraser

HARPER & ROW, PUBLISHERS

New York, Evanston, San Francisco, London

Grateful acknowledgment is made to the following publishers for permission to reprint from their limited editions of Kathleen Fraser's previous books: Kayak Books for *Change of Address*, ©1967 by Kathleen Fraser. Kayak Books for *In Defiance of the Rains*, © 1969 by Kathleen Fraser. The Penumbra Press for *Little Notes to You, from Lucas Street*, © 1972 by Kathleen Fraser.

"The Baker's Daughter," "Poem Wondering If I'm Pregant," "Casa de Pollos," "Grass," and "A Child Drowns in the Sea of Its Own Imagining" first appeared in *Poetry*.

"The Stretching Begins" and "Because of the Silence" were first published in *The Hudson Review*, Vol. XIX, No. 1 (Spring 1966).

The poems "Change of Address" and "little joy poem" first appeared in *The New Yorker*.

"Letters: to Barbara," "Soundings," and "Poem in Which My Legs Are Accepted" are from *The Young American Poets*, © 1968 by Follett Publishing Company, a division of Follett Corporation.

Some of the poems in this volume have appeared in *Kayak, The Lamp in the Spine, The Occident, Open Reading, Panjandrum, Poetry Northwest, Stooge, Sumac, Two Charlies,* and *Mademoiselle*.

Other poems have appeared or will appear in the following anthologies: *No More Masks*, © 1973, edited by Florence Howe and Ellen Bass, published by Anchor Press/Doubleday & Company, Inc.; *Rising Tides*, © 1973, edited by Laura Chester and Sharon Barba, published by Washington Square Press; and *Woman: The New Voice*, edited by Lucille Iverson and Kathryn Ruby, to be published by Bantam Books, Inc.

Library of Congress Cataloging in Publication Data

Fraser, Kathleen.
    What I want.
    Poems.
    I. Title.
PS3556.R353W5   811'.5'4   73–4081
ISBN 0–06–011342–1
ISBN 0–06–011344–8 (pbk.)

This book comes together at a time when I am particularly grateful to women who have given me paths to myself. I dedicate it, especially, to:

Marjorie Fraser, *my mother, who has always held out for joy*

Mary and Anne, *my sisters, bringing me wildflowers/vulnerability*

Ellen, *first friend, who said Yes to her self*

Maud Spicer Skolnick, *for marmalade and its glinty promise*

Dr. Marjorie White, *who listened to my pornographic dream and laughed*

Sujenna, *for the protection of salt*

Lynn, *who tried to record the mockingbird*

Judy, *who cleared space for a painted stick*

Jeannie, *surrounded by need, up all night with V. Wolfe*

Adrienne, *for the risk of being articulate*

Karene, *survivor of the absurd*

Anais, *who reminded me my life could be rich, even alone*

Alix, *whose fierceness is eclipsed only by her warmth*

Cheryl, *for telling me the truth*

Ricky, *for loving her life*

Fran, *for the gentle push*

Ruth, *who taught me acute angles and the light they bear*

Mary O, *Mary H and Mary C—for the persistence of grace*

Contents

PART II

WANTING TO BE ALL YOUR FEELINGS

(from *In Defiance of the Rains,* 1969)

PART V

JOURNAL ENTRIES

PART I

ACCESS

(from *Change of Address,* 1967)

Access

for Harry Fainlight

The man, you were the beginning of,
swilling the rain, Harry,
you had time to focus
like the knocker on a door
about to be opened.
I'm thinking how an afternoon changes,
walking towards the door without knowing
where it is,
how your jaw grinds,
imitating an effort
you cannot speak of.
Women need men to talk to.
Did you know this when we passed in the dark
and could see each other's faces?

Harry, there is someone breathing heavily
over the microphone,
our beer has foam on it,
your giving day is here and turning
on its heel.
Accidents ought to be a way of life!

The bar cleared out (did you notice?)
when I passed you my one-word vocabulary.
I said "Access" and you understood it
like the beginning of a private language,
our faces cut sharply in profile
the way an orange is sliced

3

to make a wheel that travels
by scent.

The door slams. It's later now. I'm home
and pushing you away with the groceries. But there you are,
Harry, standing on one toe on top of the Polish bar
on 4th Street. You have a cape on
and carry your anxieties
like a switchboard tangled with incoming calls.
Don't answer them!

To take a stance means having to grow still
before moving.
So you've entered the walking contest.

I can hear you weaving with love, from bar
to bar.
You have passed from the light rain into dark,
signaling me by your moving jaw
from a great distance.

The walker takes off his shoes
when he comes to grass. It's enough.

Little Poem for Frank

Yes. To run up. Yes, across this glass
my watery smile is fake. What I want is.
But more than that.
(I have real teeth, but am lacking method.)
The things I want to say have to do with love.
I think you have many shelves
but never put love there.
I am warmed when
you walk to the stove in your blue jeans.

The Baker's Daughter

Personal things is all I care about, she said.
He wouldn't be personal.
That's why I changed hearts. Parts of me ache.
But when *our* legs touch
I know what *we* have in common. We loving two.
And pancakes, the joy they bring, is what I wanted to tell most.
We made a crack in the wall to whisper through.
That's personal.
Or the dream, his skin full of blood. You've been crying, I said.
I gave him sympathy because I wanted sympathy from him.
I thought I was good. But it was lonesome.
I woke up full of lonesome. I wanted to be personal.
So I lit the oven. She said.

Reaching-Out Poem

You cut your hair and it made me very shy.
I wondered if you were rich that year you pretended
to be poor. I wanted to please you.
Do you know how many days I thought of it?
Your hair as a roof
might have been a comfortable relationship
but now that you've grown it we don't speak
the same language. I don't care about the alphabet,
only accents. If a person's from Oklahoma,
I assume we understand each other. If I said to you,
"Hey you'n down yonder in that sharp outfit,"
you might smile if you had been a child there.
But I keep forgetting history. My Colorado friends
climbed mountains together. The hunt.
All that meat cut and wrapped in butcher paper
and stored for winter in the town freezer.
Elk steak. Venison roast.
If I sang "Live Wires for Jesus," a whole line of
pictures would start moving through their heads,
drawn in crayon, at tables in the church back room
where it was cold.
I am talking about understanding. And I think
my life has gone wrong. I mean wanting the wrong
things, but not even admitting it.

Ships

"Now you're showing me you can use the language
Yet did you understand?
                              smoke   nails
          are you able to unbury the ship?"
                              —BARBARA GUEST

Introducing my exterior
it was blue yes and smooth oh
you liked it
for no rough edges,
you thought you'd order a dozen
in different colors,
                    ports `
where you could secure your ship
sailing
in over smooth, dark waters.

You rocked, captain,
you rocked and felt your edges.

My own ships, oh my beautiful hot angers
so long I have hidden you—
steamships with tin boilers ripping,
or the endless cellars of wine
on the ships of France.
I taste you and drink
to breaking of smooth waters,
to flat dark stretches
now choppy,

ports skipping with foam,
                with birds
that follow for garbage
                thrown from the deck.

The Mover to Be Moved Through

for the dancer Yvonne Rainer

1

      Put your foot down
solid
      and the other foot
follows.
      Is it the room that
builds
      itself around you, or
you
      as the room, your
hair
      the walls straight to
shoulders,
      your eyes closing and
opening,
      windows at fingertips?

2

My madness is in you.
When I move sideways
through a room, my skin
sticks like wallpaper.
It sprouts flowers
or pretends death
is a wall
too high to climb
or see over.
But you walk directly

to the room's center.
Your skin is your heart.
You stand on your head
forcing heart attacks,
watching the floor bleed.

3

Tuesday they found
                    her white goose
with a rope
                around its neck
Thursday her red
                balloons were knifed
On Friday her man
                    wore wheels for ears
and said "no more
                love," then pulled
in his belt a notch
                    and rolled away
On Monday
                the moon arrived
The girl stood
                in her flesh
with her shadow
                    panting

The Stretching Begins

The stretching begins with the road.
Pulled out from Barcelona like brown taffy,
it knots and twists
boiled stiff for forty miles.
At St. Andrea de la Barca your tongue moves
for a moment, saying

            Andrew   the boat   the wild sea,

then grows dry as the road burns
once more into fields without water.
Later when the bus stops, you taste the silence
of the path, the old man who walks there,
your rented house on the far hill with its new paint
blistering.

2

Looking for the absolute, you found yourself
and were terrified.
For three weeks you rose with the animals,
filling every stucco room with flowers then
rushing to the fields for more; over your ankles vines
grew, your eyes almost blind with pollen.
But one afternoon the earth stood around you
like an empty quarry. And you said to yourself
I can hide no longer.
I am the stretching of a field with no fences.
You cannot leap over me. You cannot leave me behind you.

3

I come for new skin.
These taking hands, see? No nerve endings;
warts, calluses, debris in the lifeline.
Sun, crack me!

Listen. Part of me
falls. My bones are bare
and wet. A new skin is breathing
and it hurts.

Casa de Pollos

The August wind rides Spain tonight in a fierce saddle,
its maddened spurs of weather jabbing me on
to the chicken lady's house, where the inside roof is pink
and the rafters hang with yellow feet of hens,
the silenced beaks, the glazed eyes of young cocks.

I pass through her door; the chicken lady darts
through the room in a trail of blood and dries
her red hands on a splattered apron front.
Her collar is a ruff of white feathers that fits
tightly around her neck, screws her eyes
to quick yellow jots of chicken feed.
"We celebrate love, tonight," I tell her,
clutching my purse with its coins for sweet chicken.
"We want rooster flesh tonight," I say,
tasting its strut already, and its hot blood.

Her hands are yellow claws. She carries them
to the coop, concealed like weapons,
and curls them around the neck of a shrieking cock.
"The wind is a white chicken wing," she says,
"for death to flap in on. But I carry the knife."

Change of Address

When the ring gleamed white and your chair hugged the edge
of it
and I led an elephant into the tent
with my skin like gold lamé and black mesh snaking
the length of my legs and hair of pomaded waves curling red
to the waist; when I leaped to the back of the elephant,
scaling his five thousand wrinkles,
yes, feeling his huge bones lurch
and the canvas ripping up
night near my neck (and all the lights blazing);
when I slid down his hairy trunk
to lie flat in the sawdust under the five-cloved foot,
waiting, with the old silk handkerchief over my face,
did you think you were at a circus?

Or the year I wore purple velvet and a torn wedding veil
with a little blue fan spread over my pale thighs
and hovered near the ceiling pouring tea (and good omens
were predicted when the oatmeal cookies were passed)
and you cried out: The recipe, the recipe!
And then when I hitched a ride on that Spanish rooster, waving
good-bye with one hand, the other holding tight to his blazing
comb, and seven candles burned on the wedding canopy—
did you think it was a painting you were looking at?

You can tear up your lecture notes now, erase every phone
number
under my name and go shopping in someone else's suitcase.
I've changed my address again. And don't waste your money
on bilingual road maps. After a six-day ocean voyage,

a train ride and three Metro transfers you'd only find nights
where the breath churns to snow after dark
and a bench with a man making blankets of his arms, his wife
in her black wool nightgown and a three-legged cat
in her lap. And then would you know me?

November, in the Year of War

there is his jaw and also his red-rimmed eyes
and when I think of war,
which is every day now, I am most terrified
of losing the curve
of his back which I hang onto, or the warm foot,
or standing today
at the window, laughing that the air is clear,
trying not to think
of fire, of faces without bodies, rolling in
on the rising wave.

Reading the Poet Ai Ching

1

Ai Ching, exile on a Chinese plain
where all has turned against you but the wild thing,
a mountain away, your father plants trees
and bud-time moving nearer.
Ai Ching, with a girl's shivering hair
I come wondering at this wildness for ocean
that puts us in the same circle.

2

In the distance,
to see you combed, mane-deep, to the back of a horse
is to see a mountain, a sky,
the ground lifting under four hooves
and a sun behind clouds like wet metal.
Also, you give me sandals which are somehow soothing
in their odors of leather.
But joy in the wild thing, most of all.
I had forgotten riding bareback, the trees
fighting death for my hair.

3

Today we bury the old ways,
together, by water,
the wild skies near Kwangtung flooding your eye,
my sky rushing from butterfly trees near Monterey,
three thousand miles in the distance.
Look! The coin I fevered for is so weightless it floats.

Grass

for Jon

Grass! That's my grass
green poking
cool in hot summer and
yellow under the washtub.
From there I've seen
stars falling. The grass is
my second skin. Drawers opening,
spilling with green.
Or doors. Each blade
the entrance to the grass city.
Lie in it. Open slowly to it.
The creatures moving there
are among endless waving forests
of green. Their tasks, cool
as through tinted glass.
Moving along the natural order.

The names of grasses
have their own smell:
beach grass
beard grass
Bengal grass
bent, bent grass
running barefoot grass
Eric Satie grass
Bermuda, back bent, bluegrass
bluejoint and bog grass
bristly foxtail

bunch grass in bunches
canary grass singing
China grass, ping!
and tiny figures floating in it
cocksfoot grass with splayed talons
cotton grass, cotton grass
crab grass, claws and colors
eel grass, green grass
English rye and feather grass
finger grass for slipping hands on
fly-away grass, with-me grass
four-leaved grass with leaf plans
gama, sesame
grama grass

guinea grass for shilling
shalling
hairgrass washed by the rain
hassock grass, the resting place
Japanese lawn grass
sprouting calligraphy
Kentucky bluegrass with
horses and riders
little quaking grass
(what does the green fear?)
love grass I love you
meadow grass will bury me
myrtle grass, orchard grass

pampas grass/oh who shall ride there?
pepper grass and pepper-grinding

pony grass where colts are born
ribbon grass by yards and inches
for necklaces and the ankles of girls
squirrel tail grass with
small eyes blinking in it
grass called star
grass with stripes
sword grass, inflictor of pain
and Tears for Timothy
the boy who said Yes
tufted hair grass
from hiding in fields and
woolly beard grass
on the chin of the hill.
Oh yellow-eyed grass has known
laughing and whirling
and the stalk of the zebra,
the stalk of the zebra.

A Child Drowns in the Sea
of Its Own Imagining

No taller than the grass
she swims in a sea
that is wet and green behind the house
where nothing moves
but the wash. It is Monday.
The only noise is of bees
spinning webs in the sky,
and she's sitting bare
with her skin pressed green
to the ground, faint shapes
of pigeons flying through her eyes
and a dream of fine ladies
bathing.
The idea in her head is to swim,
an impulse of pulling clothes down,
of skirts spread over the sea.

Oh coolness of legs Oh
lettuce and clover morning.
There are waves of dew on the lawn
and my mother is coming.
My mother is coming to chase the sea
with a towel. She shakes
questions all over the grass.

Dresses

Twelve and ugly
always wearing hand-me-downs
(O beautiful dresses I cannot have you)
and Mrs. Brown
"went to town, with her panties hanging down,"
deaconess of my father's church in Tulsa.
Bringing boxes of old clothes,
she called them presents for me,
muddy bumpy ladies' dresses,
the kind you pin brooches on
between the bosoms (or breasts
as it said in Song of Solomon that summer).
Mrs. Brown being Christian,
inviting me to milk her cows
in the country. Three days in the country.
Mrs. Brown saying "It is hot, dear,
wouldn't you like to take off all your clothes
while the men are away?"
Afraid to say no,
I wore my underwear and hated her
lying wrinkled and naked in the sun on her bed.

Hurt that I wanted to go home,
she never sent presents after that.
But other boxes came. Other people's clothes—
faded, too tight in the hips or saggy on top.
"It looks lovely, dear," they would say, dreaming
of their kindnesses, how Christ would forgive them if
he came to earth and found them sitting
in the movie house on Sunday.

(O beautiful dresses I cannot have you)
Ribbons pink and blue satin
streaming from the hair of Ginger Stinson who let boys
kiss her and was popular.
Maroon velvet curtains in the gymnasium
hiding games behind them—*Phantom of the Opera.*

When I was a child I spoke as a child
I thought as a child I understood
as a child.
But how does one put away childish things?

Poem in Which My Legs Are Accepted

Legs!
How we have suffered each other,
never meeting the standards of magazines
                    or official measurements.

I have hung you from trapezes,
        sat you on wooden rollers,
            pulled and pushed you
            with the anxiety of taffy,
and still, you are yourselves!

Most obvious imperfection, blight on my fantasy life,
strong,
plump,
never to be skinny
or even hinting of the svelte beauties in history books
                        or Sears catalogues.
Here you are—solid, fleshy and
white as when I first noticed you, sitting on the toilet,
                spread softly over the wooden seat,
having been with me only twelve years,
                        yet
as obvious as the legs of my thirty-year-old gym teacher.

Legs!
Oh that was the year we did acrobatics in the annual gym show.
How you split for me!
                    One-handed cartwheels
                    from this end of the gymnasium to the
                                        other,

                    ending in double splits,
legs you flashed in blue rayon slacks my mother bought for the
                                                        occasion
and though you were confidently swinging along,
the rest of me blushed at the sound of clapping.

Legs!
How I have worried about you, not able to hide you,
embarrassed at beaches, in high school
                    when the cheerleaders' slim brown legs
                                    spread all over
                                    the sand
                                    with the perfection
                                    of bamboo.
I hated you, and still you have never given out on me.

With you
I have risen to the top of blue waves,
with you
I have carried food home as a loving gift
                                    when my arms began un-
                                    jelling like madrilène.
Legs, you are a pillow,
white and plentiful with feathers for his wild head.
You are the endless scenery
behind the tense sinewy elegance of his two dark legs.
You welcome him joyfully
and dance.

And you will be the locks in a new canal between continents.
The ship of life will push out of you
and rejoice
in the whiteness,

in the first floating and rising of
water.

Sad Poem

for Murray and Amy

A sudden empty place
where something was.
I had just put sausage
and beans in the clay pot
thinking to make soup for you.

Now you are not on your way.

A letter with so many misspelled words
tells me you are hurrying
towards your life
in a different direction
than the one we planned
          on a calm night
          without danger.
How unpredictable,
what calls to us in a safe room
filled with the furniture we collect
to reassure ourselves.

In a dream, the furniture disappears.
There are only windows and a single door
with an arrow
          pointing to the forest.

You are not coming.

Glass

My relationships have become glass
with the clarity
of windows that are very clean.
Through the glass
        I can see you
        and my need for you.
It is shining
the way sun does on those fat blue days
of sky everywhere.
How much simpler to live in a house with dirty windows,
leaving a thumbprint
in the dust, now
       and then,
           small clues
to sustain the fact of us.
In that house, all is covered
          lightly,
with delicacy.
      Each feels his own strength
move in him
but would wear dark glasses to shield himself,
as the dust on windows
masks the light.
Knowing you in the dim light,
      loving the half light,
how safe it felt
      to see only partly.

Song for a Man in Doubt

for Jack

The sweet cake tongue
oh women are grounded in the stuff of

without apologies
I offer myself, a thing to hang onto

a place to detour the eye that turns
in on itself

all that space a man makes
impassable with pulleys

Look
you touch my arm and you've touched

all of me, waves inside my skin
The talk of dark places

becomes a conjecture
except as it is the shadow of

or the hollow in
(it has ends it has beginnings)

I am here to fill and be filled
My feet grab the soil like radishes

Because of the Silence

for R. K.

Hands on the screen door,
unable to open it. Six weeks
of silence, then pressure.
Feeling hollows in me now,
cold grays of Maymonth near
the end when it rains afternoons.
I am lonely for my life.
And think there is hope
in naming you, as you stand
by the Hudson in winter,
large and wool-wrapped,
listening to the ice move,
listening
to your heart move.
How do you live with the weight
these times? Dive under
ice, submerge, bathe in,
become the rush of water?
My heaviness can't remember how
to float.

On Sunday, intending to mount
and ride for an hour, I
wandered, waiting for the horse
to return from running free
in the hill grass.
There was a cage of peacocks
behind the barn, a male and female

circling beyond the wire.
He had spread his erotic fan,
holding back nothing. Peacock
blue, the feathers shook
and connected, desiring to dazzle
her—eyes darting black
from blue. His stiffened neck spoke
a beautiful intention.
She was oblivious,
digging the dirt with
her claws, pecking at corn.
I found them so and wanted
to yell "Fool" at her.
Then the horses came
and I rode a brown one
straight into the forest,
hoping to touch my life.

Thirst

Moving from Monday
                    to Tuesday, liquidly
the thin and shining spatula
cutting through egg white
the undulance of again
                    and again
                    rain,
full of gutters, my only life-sign
the rising of hair on both arms
when
        the startled rat leaps
                    and claws
at my entry into the night world.
Darkness, I miss you
                    but also am
                    relieved.
My shoulder blades carry a calmness.
No need to etch my name on the moon,
yet the sun
when it comes
                    is like butter.
                    It seasons everything,
                        adds richness. . . .
How can I deny it?
To be a conscious plant.
It is not enough:
                    drinking water,
                    ridding myself of poison.
Better, a starving dog with no pedigree,
wiggling its hind parts.

From a Place Not Home

In my legs, a shining
string of fireworks pulled up
through the veins
                and exploding—
your letter brings me this cry
against gravity
                (the body's swing down).

Late afternoons are the worst.
Gas fumes flood the windows,
                a pipeline of
truck exhausts loving my lungs.
I lie on the bed
                wishing for home,
                for familiar anxieties.
The exotic has become dull
my fingers are more interesting.
How long can I be calm?

This city is against itself
so how may I enter?
                No longer ingenuous or a satisfaction
                of leafy trees.
Something is dead here
and I cannot give it breath from
                my mouth.
Rooms, windows, familiar ugliness
of the violent life,
        when will I embrace you?

34

Song for a Girl, Gone

the new shoe of me, Miranda,
empty under your bed, but warm still
for a foot to fit

my loose toes, my toes wanting leather
a pull of laces
or scruffs and wearing-thins
from walks over stones

Miranda, your long, long hair and
the chair you wanted to see the sky from
(it is suddenly wider and full of light)

where does the shoe go, where does it go?
"if the shoe fits, wear it"
straight to your heart
where the windows are boarded up

the old shoe filled with fear
the mud shoe. The shelf where we shall attempt
new formulas and repairs

     saddle soap, sponges
     water, rags, brushes

the supple makers and rich bringers
the heart made pliant, old leather heart
a measure of kindness each day

and a pencil of my own to avoid the literal

Blues for Sylvia

With all my fine teach taught, I pared me down.
Nothing I am now—
a clean floor on Saturdays or water in the tank.
Sadness invades me with old-fashioned weapons,
rust marks nobody finds exciting.
I am a file cabinet, all process makes me essential
but where did I go
and who calls for me in the midnights.
I remember being beautiful,
it smelled good.
He liked me so much the others were shadows
in the sheet game;
we sat and watched them together,
but I was his light and his projector.
Suddenly I have years and no babies,
empty shelves that used to creak from
so many plans.
I'm clean as a toothbrush now
and familiar as a mouthful of teeth.

Blues #3

Each day that I turn away
from myself, I take
a step backwards.
Look,
how the hour gets fat
like a vein
hardening from lack
of exercise, from the rich
white fat of animals
glossing my inside narrowness,
the channels of the body
always moving—
is it forwards or
backwards from the heart?
Today I will comb my hair.
Shall I make the bed?
Today I will put on my green velvet
dress with the glass beads tossing
against it.
Today my name is Sylvia,
name like a river.
I can float in it
forever. Or drown.
Or move my arms
though the water makes the velvet soggy,
as if my life were that weight
on my limbs, pulling.
As if. And is.
The truth is I am lost,
& have misplaced my list

of accomplishments.
My father disappeared on the road
four months ago.
Then my first child,
the size of a tulip bulb
still buried in winter,
left me for the river.
I feel lonesome
and have no plan.

The Warning: Blues #4

Now the dream comes
two nights in a row.
Now the dream comes
with a familiar man in it.
He may be standing
on the other side of a door.
He may be closing the window.
When I see him, there is no escape,
although he is simple
and without visible weapons.
He stands there quietly
and my life is threatened.
Now I know how it feels
to be given one year to live.
There is no heroism.
Plans evade me like trees
quickly photographed.
Many branches, all reaching away
from this particular place.
The sky a white glare
and nothing to swing from.
But I'm not looking for the miraculous.
Except that
I love my life. It is all I ask for.
The man, clothed humanly,
stands with a vacant stare.
He is my enemy.

PART II

WANTING TO BE ALL
YOUR FEELINGS

(from *In Defiance of the Rains,* 1969)

In Defiance (of the Rains)

So very staunch. So.
Quiet.
Solidly, her. (the essence)
Except that to conceal like a little cup
of sanity, she is careful.
Domesticity, how white!
"but there are eyes in me," see.
And want. "they need fingers."
In a closet in an unfurnished room all claws
are bitten consistently
in the rhythm of trouble.
But love grows sharper points.

He brings me a dandelion gone to seed
and wants me to blow it and wants his way.

Sincerity keeps
hearing itself (heaviness
like a wall) and begs off . . .
to make a loud tear in an old
expensive fabric
unplanned and desperate of course
but bright as in wit,
as in blade.

They said when the diamond merchant loved me
my skin sparkled authentically.

But I had turned my back on big business
at an early age. Though the evidence

reveals
that he knew where the jewels were.
She said, "They seemed to glitter
just because his eyes were wide upon me
in thirst. And I could afford to be
well-manicured."

Yet the awareness, and under it
a further cluster of words like a dab of paint
you watch your hand place
with the brush (not used enough)
and the paint drying in tubes.
To explode.
All the new flash.

He wanted her pen to write poems in the grass.

Memoirs of a Saint

for Magritte

I cannot doubt
all that blue
unfolding,
a sky of puffs.
The sentiment
saves me.
Erotic
sharks swim the
under-
side of the sea.
Now curtains
open neatly above them
(pleats
to the left
and the right).
How the apple says
tart!
Perfidious green
and roundness,
endless. Its stem
snaps; the ceiling
cracks
with pressure.
I am saved
from perfection.
The smallest gestures
love me.

Letters: to her

for Mary Fraser, 1943–1969

You have taken your hands from your ears.
I'll sweep away the dead skin.
I'll bring ointment.
Your reward is to hurt. Your reward
is to add a name after the name you were given.
Your clothes will no longer fit you
and your hair may fall into the lake.
I rejoice for you
as you put your fear into the drawer,
as you enter the sorrow
of one and then another
like a transfusion of type O.
You want to change your mind
but the river goes one direction
and you have entered the rapids.
Dangerous waters. Rocks. Music of clarity.
Then quite suddenly, the ocean . . .
and you learn the meaning of fish.

Letters: to Barbara

Why must my life be as obvious as an elbow?
Feelings stick to me like expensive glue—
adhesive, persistently
not pulling away for years.
Little words and big words are flying,
are flying. Red exotic birds
in a history I ooh over, myself above the page,
a wishful face with tear ducts under the bones.
Good bones
I've been told. High. And skull
following the fitter dictates of survival.
Will my child inherit this measurement
and myself the pain?
Do you know what I mean? This plenitude
of silence. This fullness and emptiness.
This stranger who moves wherever I move.

Letters: to him

Can't we pretend there were monsoons
and they're done with.
The sun's out.
And love is melting you,
ready to force its way as abundantly
as the roses do, making an arc
through the cracks of David's window . . .
he smiles when I show him
how they arrive every morning
in red bursts.

I know you must be writing me. I can feel
all those words getting lost in your head
and floating—rafts of balsam and apricot
wood, all awkwardly nailed
and smelling of the delicious odors
your hands give off. These complications
of love, of leaving.
The blood asks questions and we are impelled,
in spite of subtleties.

Letters: to J and D

You appeared like a tidal wave
rising at my window.
Now you recede
with the sadness of low tide,
and if I am a shore
there is dampness still to touch,
new bits of wood washed up
to remind me of your absence.
O blond and rust-colored friends,
your frying pan sputters with
fish sliding over greased metal.
Surely it is holy,
this hunger we share. See
how the stove anticipates our fire
and the salad abundantly brings forth
fresh mushrooms new to your tongue.
No regrets, but appetite rising
as I envision you
speeding through brussels sprouts
avoiding their soggy tradition.
My pen feels glamorous with energy.
I can't run out of ink and
I send you a gift of it.

Nasturtiums

All the muscles of my forehead
lean in
and lock
      to grip you
            now that you're leaving.
Why?
When your bodies touched so lovingly
on the rug.
Two nasturtiums. That bright.
With green
qualities, leafy
as we stretched in the forest and
your hearts became pine
            at the top parts.
Oh friends, we need more trees! Don't go.

Your lust for sleeping bags' softness
calls
and the highway south. Small fish.
Still,
I entreat you, old-fashionedly:

           prepare your lasso
           with speed and hunger,
           I'm looking for a hill.

Will you burn there,
our words
      throw out lines
           to the sea?

Poem Wondering if I'm Pregnant

Is it you? Are you there,
thief I can't see,
    drinking,
    leaving me at the edge
    of breathing?
New mystery floating up my left arm,
clinging to the curtain.
    Uncontrollable.
Eyes on stalks, full of pollen,
stem juice, petals making ready to unfold,
to be set in a white window,
or an empty courtyard.
Fingers fresh. And cranium,
    a clean architecture
    with doors
    that swing open . . .
is it you, penny face?
Is it you?

Gloom Song

The gloom queen   rides by
with

      THE FUTURE HANDS AND FEET

          tucked
          in her
          belly

                her horse
                is
                a rocking chair
                that
                makes her dizzy

with small white words click-clicking
against her teeth

          "What I want
          oh I want it,
         though I don't know
           what I want."

Waiting

The long pull of muscle in the back of the legs,
tunes from walking the hill at midnight.
I can feel only this physical stretching,
but otherwise blend into the room
like a piece of old furniture.
What is this gray life I continually kick from?

You are now the length of my finger.
Your head is fruit-shaped and succulent with juices.
At the edge of humanness, you are ready
to feel the blood in your wrists which are flat as fins.
I'm waiting to be needed.

O son, O daughter, where are your mysteries?
Could I have guessed it? This house, my head, so empty
and badly carpentered that boredom leaks through its rafters?
My healthy feet are waiting
to take me, oh anywhere. Arrive with your anger,
new life in me!

Poems for the New

1

we're connecting,
        foot under my rib.
I'm sore with life!
At night,
        your toes grow. Inches of the new!
The lion prowls the sky
and shakes his tail for you.
Pieces of moon
        fly by my kitchen window.
And your father comes
riding the lion's back
        in the dark,
to hold me,
        you,
           in the perfect circle of him.

2

Voluptuous against him, I am
nothing superfluous,
but all—
bones, bark of him, root of him take.
I am round
with his sprouting,
new thing new thing!
He wraps me.
The sheets are white.

My belly has tracks on it—
                        hands and feet
are moving
under this taut skin.
In snow, in light,
we are about to become!

Soundings

for Denise and Mitch

Honey! My mouth is full of it.
Honeysuckle white and yellow
trumpeting from my mouth.
Sweet blossoms, honey blossoms.

And the sea at my feet,
at my ears. It comes and goes
with its power.
Can I comment?

It moves in spite of me,
as my life does,
and I am thankful
for the clear details

that ride on its surface—
the sailboat, small and white
and pure of shape,
the honeysuckle in my mouth.

I delivered of myself
a child called David.
Six months of breath
and already he is himself,

arms stretched to the water.
His energy doesn't require me
or care that I care.

He is all of him urge.

Fearless before the sea's
sucking and unbalancing
beauty, he makes his sounds,
his respondings.

I can only guess that
there is joy in the guttural cry.
I give him honeysuckle
and he admires the whole flower,

his mouth desires it.
Neither goodness nor evil
enters into it.
The eye beholds a rushing of blue,

breaking on rocks.
The skin feels a cool wetness,
a small wind.
It wants. It wants.

Since Looking into the Mirror

this morning, a new line.
Your darkness
falling upon me
with the precise mark
of an etcher's tool.
My torn hands
are a signal I am
not observing
with proper awe.
Pieces of flesh lost
for what love,
lost?
I would do better as
your fantasy.
Then
you'd send letters,
flashes,
numbers exchanged in the night
instead of fog,
massing zeros
quietly.

Just Beyond Sight

Just beyond sight
the quivering fox makes the air alert.
Now my arm is on fire;
all the candles I bought have melted
in the sun's persistent yellow.
I am trying to work my way
through the underbrush
to tropical fruits
cut down before I can reach them.
My left hand is full of pain—
thorn
or fear
or the stains of small insects
with terrible powers.
I am tired of being strong.
My life is turning its back on me
abruptly.
With David I cry out
in the dark
and bind myself with silken threads
hoping to hold me together.
I dream of the fox.
Of his glittering.

Decoy

for Ralph Dickey

Unlike our conversations, your hands
give you away.
From the piano bench the muscles
of your back, thick
under thin cotton . . .
we can no longer make plans.
I read you as many ways as flags
are folded. You are mysterious,
the way yellow enters blue
if the wind is blowing.
You signal compulsively
and I receive you. Blindly.
I'm in love with primary color.

"To a Boat, Streets Have No Feeling"

—Joseph Ceravolo

1

I am running from poem to poem
wanting to be all your feelings,
such as: he wrote his love on a postcard
or
she noticed a scarab on the floor of her compartment
and listened hard,
unfolding herself like a set of trick playing cards
full of faces.

2

Precisely
because
the sun descends
into my legs
and melts my worde horde oh mystery!

I am high on celery and eggplant
and will bathe myself
in the green air of fresh vegetables
to celebrate our love.

3

When I transplanted the red poinsettia,
it had already grown
top-heavy, often falling over
as we passed.
In the small pot of clay

you could see its roots
all tangled with reaching
for lack of soil and space, a mass
of intricate white connections
growing into each other.

4

Between two days
an enormous space and our nudeness
or the rose petals
you gave me in a cake of soap.
The smell
of you comes in the door
and I place a tomato
cut in sharp red fours around the plate
to honor how
I leap to your old clothes
and the skin of soft inner arms.

little joy poem

Like a shiny bus in the snow,
I feel good this morning—
new upholstery, green and tough,
I'll never wear out!
The snowplow came at 2 A.M.
last night on its lonely task
and I looked from the window
waving my toothbrush.
(At night, the snow
changes color.)
Here I am—two legs
a new morning
and joy,
like the whiteness of cold milk,
filling me up.

PART III

DOOR

(from *Little Notes to You,*

from Lucas Street, 1972)

Little Notes to You, from Lucas Street

1

In Iris mud
her legs stems
and separate even
if it's afternoon by the porch

2

Still her curls are just unwinding
from the large-size pinks
Plastics fresh as spring
Mud rushes up in her throat

3

There's a song she's trying
to remember she knows
it's there   Her boys are there
on each muddy bike

4

Red paint and blue paint
bicycles   The sun's
the sun's out as a presence
of snow running

5

I don't know
where I am   Bread rises and smells

Only half an inch
of pink detergent and my hands
compose with two oranges

6

Is my mouth a pocket?
Its mystery
a presence as separate as the porch
The children in our puddle
walk reverently
in green and red sweat shirts

7

Somewhere a switch disconnecting
Along the white edge of
snowlight nothing hurts
Call me with your danger

8

Red deep red,
anemones purple anemones
We watch them float
somewhere near the center of the table
Anne is getting married
The petals' dark tensing center

9

Are you the mysterious presence?
One always waits
The possible new thrill
could be licking a stamp

10

Long glossy cars at ease in the parking zones
always gliding through the temporary zones
stopping firmly before the non-stop zones
Their confidence tilts
the only balance one has mastered

11

No, was it lovely? Really?
Seeing again
The tension stretched so exquisitely pale
it almost disappeared behind love
And the one thing you never tell me

12

Your knees move in spite of you
They reveal your hair, the shape
of your fear   On the bus
we showed off our children   See,
I can play mommy and daddy

13

The sniper lurked as I thought of
taking off my blouse for you
You sniffed him   reared up
My hair got more beautiful as you looked

Now

you are where you are

a presence of swimmer's hair falling

and you smell of your mouth & the night
all over your boots

on the step, through the door, falling upon me

your body refuses my poem
will not fit
but springs from the dark with an overpowering scent

something I cannot track in myself
watches you watching

this is where
we begin   in heavy rain

in wet leaves my feet push
to your joy running   ahead of you
flexing and articulate as branches you recognize
one at a time

flowers begin to take sharp bites of you
out of sequence

you are amazed
and worry,
yet can almost shed your skin with its old rupture

you are breathing deeply
I inhale you through your loose clothing
where there is space to feel myself

growing small with a kind of beast shyness

I inherit you as a resonance
who fully inhabits
the field I have taken years to clear

Loving

for Dick

knock last night's softness
of snow, of snow
off the green wood sticks

knock on the stove
to let us in

we make fires, fires go

and even when we walk away
from snow,
we are tending what remains

we bank coals, breathe
ourselves into them,

pile wood against the hour we cannot name

warmth is where
we touch the bones of each
other

Love Poem Written in the Swimming Pool

Recreation Center, Iowa City

An endless flow of white cells—
the public address system sticks to my skin
with wet cloth of popular music/
the fifties
waxing my ears with its thick yellow.

I slide into blue water
to escape the predictable
and my body shocks
with tiny stings of chlorine.

Side. Stroke. Side. Stroke. Side. Stroke.

I believe in slow beginnings.

Now I'm turning. Now I'm loving
the stretch and wake of muscles
learning their awkwardness,
back to back with the blue length.

I am hungry and want to eat the tiles,
the silver metal curves
that pull people up
to the safety of towels,

to drink
the pale, shimmering gallons,

move through them as flawlessly as music does
through this swimming pool air.

But the brain stutters its bit of data
from last year's drowning,
sends messages I'm unwilling to decode.
Still, a watchfulness wires my lungs—
the ghost of water in combat with
water.

Then you are there. On the ceiling, I mean.
Your face
is pacing mine. Your arms are streaking
with neon and your tender mouth
gives off the contained silence of noiseproof ceilings
where thought is roared.
I see you.
Am entered.
And swim effortlessly. My body changed. Flowing.

Wishing My Typewriter Were a Piano

Keys, if you were attached to catgut, a vibration of animal whose
cry
is a keening . . .

but you are single windows,
showing O to suggest the sound I cannot make,
striking D for the man who hides and seeks in the small places
of my mouth,
clearing to K which is myself who has been pure light,
now curling against the changing weather, throat raw with
expectation.

You lack the mystery of unknown scales, are precise with each
stab
of my fingers, commit me to the blush of my own yearning.

Are you giving me your real thoughts? How can I know?

(He told me of looking at the woman he was to marry, of
understanding his hate
for her, of smiling . . . was it that smile tucked into my drawer this
morning?)

If you were a piano and my hands tuned,
keys, I would play the clear notes of black and white
and Mendelssohn would listen. The notes would sing of my
doubt.

"Respect Is Not to Assume Too Little"

—Alexandra Colt

And I assumed too little,
kept
packaging you
with gravity,
trying to design space
like a shelf
I could measure,
placed us neat there—
two pairs of shoes.

And I assumed
a small sameness in you,
a smaller difference,
calming my future with less
and less,
provoking
your mysteries, elbows
you had barely uncovered,
knitting sweaters
in the nighttimes,
fearing how they did not fit
what I knew.

And you assumed too little,
planted me,
potted me how it felt good to you.
That answer,
yourself as gardener,

sustained you
until I began
growing ungainly offshoots.
My urges
needed a changing yellow
light of much
thought.
I heard the red clay
cracking.

And you assumed
a small sameness in me,
a smaller difference.
And went your ways
not wanting to look
at my sorrow taking root.
I learned not to weep.
My head shaped to a hand
and I began digging.

Letter to Sun Valley

I heard your boots cry out
this morning when my blue Chevrolet
leaped the Dodge St. bridge just above the railroad cars
where Patrick and Ruth once laid their cold, loving bodies.

Your skis cracked.
Your toothbrush fell from its hidden pocket
and the *Dipladenia splendens,* green from your green hand,
in full sun unfolded its five pale mysteries for me
like delicate pink babies
calling into question your departure with their energy.

Inside me, the puzzle of how you often go.
Idaho is missing from David's map of the States.
I've tried to remember its color and have looked under all the
                                                    chairs
for an unknown shape,
but the same gray space stares back.
It insists on moving into me

though I've spent my life resisting geography.
In spite of this, I begin to think of Idaho potatoes
and one lovely valley. Is it there you will feel your skin
split, slip off a notch at a time, leaving all of it behind you
finally, moist and new, riding sunlight like an untethered pony?

Door

The wood takes your hand on it
for granted, the squeak is the door's condition,
the push is your body against it
and when you have moved through infinite
motions involving wrists, nerves, rough skin of hands
that weld you to whatever you touch,
then you are more than the picture of you
coming through the door, now the body of you, the voice
hello, hello, the smell along your neck—
yet another layering and way of entering this room
where my hands slide among tin things, pottery
water and bubbles, slippery with a purpose
of making new. Clean surfaces & this flash
of order tilting to collapse.
Dishes, kitchens, and you still moving
through the door, hard man and softly there,
complexity of a simple idea. My mind has generated
sunlight since waking, has rained on you, pulling you
out of fiction, making memory a real and pungent soil.
Belief slowly germinates love. And love seeps,
takes oxygen and light. Light becomes the green shape
of tiny leaves pressing out. Love is sprouts,
tastes authentic and fresh.

With Slowness

1

the pig's back against planks
                    (it cried harm)
from the tar paper roof
we heard the dripping of last furrows

which hasn't been repeated yet

2

and if you'd arrived on foot
and if you'd gone into the shed
Only three spokes of the wheel and a rind

peeled with slowness

3

would the intimacy
again
break into the air
                    as fruit does
                    (just the merest scent tells us)

I think your brain divides into summer and winter
and summer hurts

4

though I am a lake and bluer every August

5

and freezing and thawing have become so habitual I no longer
like them
enough
to spend time in their improvement

I'd rather skate to the mystery I cannot talk about

Hunger

Hunger trots and trots
over acres of the moon.

Now they have nothing
to eat. The hare's soul

is a special diet for
the sicker ones, and

whatever leaks out
is begotten in burlap

sacks. Under the moon's
influence, a lot

of bodies smelling.
We bury them and

name them according to
the places they'll haunt.

Six under my window,
obscurely intimate,

dwell in trees
and will die with them.

Sun, Three Rays

putting out its minimum
the sun

each ray like a pale metal hook
drawn through water
to illuminate

so slow
you can barely measure
its moving/as

his attention
going out of
focus

though eyes open
blankly in front of you

Agnes

1

She wouldn't like Agnes to be
like some types today.
As for the boys,
she didn't mind what boys Agnes went out with,
what boy she . . .
ummm . . .
provided he intended to marry her.
And was not flighty.
She had never objected to Agnes
kissing.
Boys.
It was natural
provided
it wasn't done openly.
Openly.
Agnes kissing.
That . . . ummm . . . was Agnes's business.
She would not interfere
unless, of course, unless
he wasn't Agnes's type.

"I hear him. He comes to my bed at night
carrying his box of plumbing tools."

"I suppose it's not quite a nice thing
to have sexual feelings, is it, do you think?
I wanted to be like Jesus,

aboveboard and straightforward.
But people are nosy. People are underhand.
Jesus helps me. But now I don't tell my mum
about the plumber."

2

Coming on since Christmas.
We had to choose our words carefully.
Agnes was sitting by the fire
putting cream on her face. I saw the fire
on her face. She was sitting there.
The cream was spread all over her.
"Oh do be careful, Agnes," her dad said.
Then she threw the tissue into the fire.
That's when it began.
Yes it had been coming. Coming on
since Christmas. Coming.

3

Agnes keeps to herself.
That's the trouble.
The illness kept coming.
She wanted to dress mannish. The disgusting way
people dress today. Kept coming.
"I wanted to wear blue jeans like Shirley and Betty
wear them. To tell the truth, men do seem
to find them attractive. Blue jeans."

Agnes was . . . ummm . . . she is always
imagining atmospheres, how people feel.

Being critical. Not liking her. And it is very trying.
The feeling people are against her.

She often masturbated when people weren't kind.
She told it to Mum.
But Mum was embarrassed.
Agnes told her about the stunt.

But Mum knew nothing about it.
There had never
been anything like that. She didn't
really know what it was. Her Mum said
"She's been spoiled more than the others.
Too much affection showered."
She tended to sense atmospheres.
Mum had always said that about Agnes.
Religion was always her trouble.
"Jesus has helped me a lot. But he's too much in my life.
He drives me. And it gets on my nerves.
But Jesus loves me. He is the only one who cares."

4

And nothing's wrong with the other two.
And nothing's wrong with the other two, Dad says.
They were just like normal persons.
Nothing seemed to worry them. Like normal persons.
Too much fuss over Agnes.
Something definitely wrong with Agnes.
She always got worked up to a point, Agnes did.
Agnes being irritable at home.

Agnes getting on our nerves.
Agnes worrying about things. Going on about things.
Agnes not mixing with everyone and anyone.
Agnes talking about religion in a simple manner.
Agnes saying her father was picking on her.
Agnes not telling her father her thoughts.
That's her illness. That's what I mean.
Agnes laughing to herself.
Agnes not pulling herself together.
Agnes liking a boy and not knowing if she's in love with him.
Agnes off to hospital.

5

50 insulin comas.
Apparently well.
Discharged.
Referred.
Relapsing.
Re-referred.
50 insulin comas.
Tranquilizers.
Discharged.
Re-admitted.
Tranquilizers.
Clinically improved.
Discharged.
Tranquilizers.

6

Dad is disappointed in Agnes.
What he wanted for her was
"Nothing nicer
than to come home from a hard day's work
and relax
and sit down
and listen to the wireless
or television
with a nice fire."
That's what he wanted for her.
With a nice fire.
What he wanted.
But no. She didn't, did she. She didn't
come home to it. No.
She'd been a failure.
He didn't mind Agnes being cheeky,
but she wasn't cheeky like other people.
She was old enough to know whether or not she was in love
with the electrician. But she didn't know.
He had been working in their house.
She heard his voice at night. But she didn't know.
Sometimes he said he would kill her, but his voice
was loving. That's why she couldn't know her true feelings.
He asked if she was married.
He asked how she spent her time.
He offered to take her to a club.
Walking down the sidewalk, she wondered
if this was "Mr. Right." Then inside her

something funny happened inside her.
Something she couldn't describe.
But it was that night he spoke to her.
That night, in her bed.
But there you are. True enough.
There was no harm in that for a normal person.

7

She'd be sitting by the fire,
and all of a sudden she'd give a silly grin or a laugh
and I'd say "Well, what are you laughing at?"
And she'd never tell. She'd never once tell.

NOTE: "Agnes" was inspired by the work of R.D. Laing and A. Esterson in *Sanity, Madness and the Family*.

Yellow

for Stephen's palette

Butternut, crooked-neck squash, lemon, rain slicker.
I am giving you my grapefruit, apples that grow gold
and cherries with the pigment of daffodils. Painted edges
of curbs. Yolk. And a certain yellow lily, the center
of daisies. This pencil, amarillo, for you, Stephen,
who attends the announcement of light with a single pinch
of saffron. Dandelions, buds of electric joy, curry
in your hair and a wife balanced on one hand
whose smile is a new season of radiance. Olé!
The afternoons are changing like a painting where the sky
eats everything in orbit. Bird! Trapeze! Heart!

Day and Night

for M. C. Escher

My eye rises in the white duck's
eye. I ferment. Extend
myself, itself
into a flat kiss of feathers.
I am duck,
and look! The city's below me, unrolling
itself like a black flag.
For death?
The chessmen will tell,
sitting with their backpacks near the king's bedroom
whose light at the windows is excessive.
Now duck, beak, wing
become ducks, beaks, wings. I am two,
in flight next to myself,
pursuing
one flight code, spitting out its digits inside me.
Going backwards now, going in threes now:
two of me clear duck,
the third me, shape and outline of duck,
with details of fields scaled on my wingtips,
furrows, pockets of seed, a few thistles
all delicately pulled along each wing.
Now four. Now four.
The sound of Quack moves out
of black ink. Four. More.
But less of what you can see.
Me, duck me sliding so very gently
into the fields of pure shape.

Now I am plots of land—shoe peg corn
and the black mud China pigs go snouting in.
I am something dark,
potato eyes dropped into elbow hollows.
Shadows. Four.
Shapes of tail beating tail.
Pulling space in both directions.
Now wings pivot without the slightest motion.
Organically the darkness moves in me west.
Sleek black feathers are kissing each other's softness.
Wings. Downy down.
Rain down on me
rain. The darkness of no color.
I am four black ducks. With a different code unfolding.
Being chased. Wanting not to disappear.
Now in hot pursuit of what is left of me.
The river below shines white. Tiny ships row and wave smoke.
Their flags unfurl the red yellow blue in my wing beat.

Sensing the Presence of Butterfly

Butter scales
Lepidoptera
yellow lapis lazuli
moving through the calendar in a linear massing of
forming
shedding
          caterpillar fuzz, a fine counting
of sprouts into what is coming
The colors   Wet
Monday   Moon's day   Day of worm moving
Warm   Moving
Spins a darkness of no choice

                    (Among Egyptians, the month
                    contained thirty days,
                    and how many cocoons?)

Invariably
the time of no light:
thirst:
the butterfly

                    (weeks go by—each a period
                    of seven days with no reference
                    to celestial motion)

only the chrysalis
the reason
I do not want to see you
though I carry invitations in both pockets
wheatberries locked in tough kernels
hungry
for sunlight

(the Greeks trying to master
chaos, as described and per-
formed by the calendar)

(Civil life/a tensing to serve
ungainliness)

(the tight-lipped relief of
my neighbor tearing the wild
growth of ivy from my window
where the butterfly poised)

Premonition blinds me
Be my cane no longer!
I grow by touch, feel the walls of my own making
from the inside   The darkness is braille
cuts sharply into my fingers
I bleed and let go

But the center stays   The threads around my body
are dry and light
What held me to the ground is gone
I am bursting   I am spinning
I am wings

PART IV

WHEN THE CHOICE
IS WARM

(New Poems)

The History of My Feeling

for D.

The history of my feeling for you (or is it the way you change
and are blameless like clouds)
                                reminds me of the sky in Portland
and the morning I unpacked
and found the white plates from Iowa City
broken,
            consistently surprising with cracks,
petals like new math theories smashed
                                with the purposeful fingers of chance.
I loved the plates. They were remnants from an auction
which still goes on in my head because of the auctioneer's body
and his sexy insinuations about the goods he was selling.

But to Ruth, who talked them into their thin wraps of newspaper,
what we were sharing was departure and two lives breaking
and learning
            to mend into new forms.

We had loved our husbands,
                        torn our bodies in classic ways to bear
                            children: Sammy, David, Wesley—
Now we loved new men and wept together
so that the plates weren't important and hadn't been packed
with the care I might have given had I been alone.
But Ruth was with me.

You were gone, like this storm that's been arriving and
                                                    disappearing
all morning.

I awoke to hear heavy rain in the gutters.
The light was uncertain and my feelings had grown less sure.
Last night, pinned by a shaft of pain—

                    your presence and your absence—

I knew clearly that I hated you
for entering me profoundly, for taking me inside you,
for husbanding me, claiming all that I knew

                          and did not know,

yet letting me go from you
into this unpredictable and loneliest of weathers.

The Lovers—Hesitant Their Touch
While the Fountain Gurgles

—from a painting by SUTTER MARIN

Darling, your head is slightly askew
but juniper trees lean
                    towards you anyway . . .
see how their leaves become tiny, alert faces
wondering and glowing, pushing towards your new difference
like a green wave
                    off the tide of someone's palette.
You never wore a rose in your buttonhole,
but it is there now, announcing
                              "a new life" in your cheeks,
a life that is just screaming for air as a rose does,
as a baby dangling
                    is alarmed by the joy of not knowing.
In relief, you are a fountain,
                         a man whose mouth gushes rainfall.
You splash,
make wave
          after wave after
wave precisely capped, white and foamy . . .
this ocean flows
from you,
          wets the grass near my feet
whose toes grow roots
               to draw you up beneath the soft folds of my skirt.

Though a wall has been painted between us,
my hair is so long it's tucked into your pocket.
And it's your hand
                        writing messages on mine.
Our touch is hesitant. But it is ours.

Hello

Hello Iowa City,
       it's going to be O.K.,
              but I confess to a pull towards
what might be happening
in your flat white fields with the sun orange and heavy.

Elizabeth writes me (innocently?)
that my man still floats
           in the thin mists icing your windshields.
In a dream *Time* reports him
           saying: "I am in love . . . in love . . .
           I am the condition of being."

It is hard trying to live apart from the energy in bodies that loved
                        you.

I keep wishing to go to Stephen's for dinner,
for the white slabs of fish with pineapple, oranges and lemons
making his kitchen into the palm tree where
our hearts sat
        looking at the clear blue horizon
ready to launch a first boat
           with its spinnaker saying Lift me!
It is clarity here.
I mean at this moment the sun graces us.
My window has its own tree to watch
              and a man's knee
sticks nakedly and joyously up from beneath the body of an old
                       car
he's been puttering with most of the afternoon.

103

The hallways that seemed long yesterday
                                got suddenly short
as I walked just now to pin a note on John's door.

Bits of red stand out
suggesting fruit will be here in another month
                                or at least its blossoms,
or at least the tiny sprigs of bush are growing into a deeper
                                redness each day
which makes me hold my breath
                                and seek them out.
It's going to be O.K.
Eric just left the room.
His hair was all electric gold, his cords were soft from being
                                washed a lot
and he kept running
                his tongue over his mouth.

What I Want

Because you are constantly coming to begin,
I suggest solutions
and am full of holes. See through me
when my back is turned.

A hotel is the notion of entrance
by thought. Your love is
constantly a solution,
criminally full
of no difference
when my back is turned.

I read your thoughts because
you are constantly changing and coming
through me
when my back is turned. And

I want something
for something
constantly. I am coming.

To Start

At a tremendous speed my throat makes its door slide.
Pure guesswork . . . I have lost the other

side of me. You'll see. In teeth dreams there are only three
wrong guesses. A surprise doesn't exist.

Just a guess against the door.
To think is simultaneous. I'll take another network

of teeth (by pairs) as my answer. Stars. Anymore.

Amid Mouths

1

more and more
rushes out at night
high on the still pooled joyful "do not"

blood cells
desert for signs inside me
A narrow ledge

the bouyant
with furry necks,
more and more

2

we are
what is
that the rare elegant necks
(more of them)
look attentively at
a baby us

they peer over the wooden boat,
but it is shore
starts
    To roll flapping
seaward, the heron ascends

each wing
has been rained
thin

3

that I snap
(but watch the little light)
just open
up
the dark see

a wonderful move
these very gentle whites
amid mouths

Growing Up

1

In a box I marry
and grow firm.
I fly to complacency
where hair runs by the ankle.

I pull Mother's dress. "Come down
out of each other's knees!" . . . and and
"fresh lines." (linen)

Is nothing the strength
of my wings' chain?

2

and was reminded
how oddly good the door of a bar,
our shoes' loose sod snow.

the grass learned again
how often the body leans
in a clearing.

(and another one breaks in on
the pleasure of her stare.)

But it seemed
the time.

3

I just wanted a soft green family.

Remember your family?

My family sadly grow less.

It's more difficult with maps

zipped inside. Show my face

in pink silk. A simple box.

Going

1

Through his giant photo body,
heaven's blue sea.

I am leaving and will close my tongue.

2

To and fro men
(particularly)
grow

windows.
Horizon. In.

3

Trees open in the neck &

his mother's thumb appears in
the lentil heart
flood.

If

Suppose we are a fragment?

A perfect night of immediacy
in vital places.

Up here I am the disguised flower
and you are where it came from.

To allow the hidden.
So slowly. My body.

And wouldn't you

begin
to make friends with it?

I can wait.

That Didn't

That didn't come down
> but quietly (to touch)
> as wheat grows. And shoes
in water. Here. A curving brown light
didn't drop down all around
> no center.
> No field where that touch seems
firm, almost.

Song

my little listen
with all my soil

oh please a story
you are not like

and the sea we sail
enoughenough

had I not tasted
you make me spin

but have I listened
you are not like

PART V

JOURNAL ENTRIES

The Difficulty

for L. M.

It was how to enter your house without you noticing.
How to be quiet.
To hear when the ocean came into your room at night.
How to absorb your Texas drawl—
(I pulled it up around my chin like my frayed quilt).

I told Bob there is no language for it.

And wanted to tell you.

No right word for it, though I still look.

*   *   *

she wanted you to know   she was she   in her knees
that she attempted   balance   but found none

      "I am falling."

      "Go ahead."

      "I think I am going to fall."

      "To the floor."

      "Oh, it's there."

      "Yes, the floor."

* * *

I want you to know I fell. The floor was carpeted so it was rather
                                                                easy.
I mean, flowers woven into it. Real oriental. A softness.
                                        Something not far away.
The pull of gravity. What the flowers wanted. Leaning a bit, into
                                                    each other.

* * *

What he wanted. To show me my weakness.
Weak knees. He placed a finger, rather long (as was his
                                                        body),
placed it against my shoulder & pushed & was down. I
                                            was down.
So easy. See.   Do you see?

I wanted to suck my thumb. He said Yes.
But he pulled it out. He wanted to make me angry.
He wanted me to feel unsteady. To see what was
in jeopardy. The shifting ground. Never quite me
standing up or sitting down. Their eyes round,
around me. Pulling down.

* * *

Something at odds in you. Yet occupied. Guarded and rooted.
Near the ground.

And for a woman (or shall I say for me) there is fear of this
sureness.
Though you are kind. But will not budge.
And will not budge.

So it feels foolish to try to begin to say it.
To say anything that might try to begin.

Entry 11/24/72

119

Afterbirth

You are falling backwards
                 over
                    and
                       over
                         your body through air
                         growing thin
as your flesh and the sky's
               flesh enter each other.
You loosen from the page. I watch you spread in water.
Your name
so left-handedly firm once in its awkwardness,
now black ink simply thinning out
as clouds might, getting undramatic, gauzy with winds, then not
                                there.
You telephone. I'm not home.
You're the dream a child's voice wakes me from. I feel it barely
touching my arm
               later on in the day as
another man sheds his peculiar cumulus in my house.

Entry 12/11/72

The Possibility of My Yellow Orchard Body

The possibility of my yellow orchard body
               springs open
          the space between two storms towing each other
It's recognizable
         and doesn't depend on New York City or being in love
but is a question
of choosing
or being awake when   the choice is warm

Entry 2/14/73

How I Understood You in Another Way

To take your place, Jenny came without your muscles
   or outside & attractive apertures and appendages
     (such as no penis between her legs and no scar on her
               forehead and
    no confidence of winning in tennis or skiing competitions)
       but had a way
             of making contact with herself
yet shielding the impact of what she was saying
                 from herself,
the moth inside her
       fluttering at the windshield, the white moth Jenny,
Jenny's hands of long fluttering fingers white
and the words in long streams from her throat
     passing through
     those fingers
passing through the inarticulate
        to I am lost
        and I watch me watch myself
and by Jenny saying it,
it falling upon us, opening us, making us begin
to vibrate
    as a system of muscles picking up vital information.
    . . .
    You might say we were tuned,
    or tuning in,
    or that small leaves began to form along our arms
    resembling the asparagus fern in my window whose
              shoots grow
    overnight.
There was a definite change of color in the room.

Among us, green made itself a presence,
a presence, as if it could have been the season,
but I think it was Jenny as an instrument,
whose tenuous place in
that space between the couch and the ceiling
                              spoke for how
each of us breaks into pieces yet continues to flow.

Entry 3/17/73

Detail

The bulbs among stones shooting green spikes

                                        from your desk
        was the thing that caught
        and made a rip
        in me
                when you began to show me your visible self
                . . .
something tender
        and unusual in a man's room—
                    that he should nurture in that
                                        particular way

Entry 3/17/73

A Poem Not About Passion or Romantic Hope,

but a liking it when you touched my neck
and so many others touching but your touch speaking
                                modestly but personally,
beginning to enter the space where we've looked across the room
                                and
listened to each other's words (odd, thorny plants without names
                                or easily identifiable colors and smells)—
your strangeness delights me, there is nothing familiar about
                                you,
nothing I've ever wanted or yearned towards. You are you.
        To watch your shyness as you try to cross a space between
                                us,
how you can hardly look at me, how your eyes don't gloss but
                                avert,
are confused by showing you like me . . .

You bring your dog. He saves you by jumping on me in the
                                middle of our kiss
in which you cannot conceal how your skin changes temperature
                                after we touch.

You are the first new man I have trusted for months. I feel my
                                body
unlock to you and am wondering and curious since it was nothing
                                I decided,
you were no one I thought about before you made your body
                                something
I should pay attention to.
What is it I hear? It is the trust that makes me curious.

In your words, I listen to anger
& flush with your power to feel. Also there is tenderness—
the delicate shapes of small rocks collected and placed above the
fire . . .
your severe room of dark green and thick white candles
the bed where I lay looking at you, the light of several fires
on us,
the silence, the trust in silence.

Entry 3/17/73

Rewrite

Doghairs on your coat and its navy blue glamour—
you're unraveling a picture I wanted to keep deep
and why do you keep calling when you can give me
nothing to chew on?
                    We meet in the middle of a sentence.
                    Your face is the (blank)
                            to be filled in later.
Oh, here's a room.
It could be where you kissed me and it was nice.
But no. It's a different room.
There's your past life floating through the air
                            perpetually.
And there you are, white and speechless.
You push your skin out on a set of bones that feels safe.
It's sort of polished. It promises it will glow
                                    in the dark
(but never does) (but never does).
The eyes are glass with no particular color.
You pretend there are no messages. You pretend you're selling
                                                me
something white and hemmed and folded up
in a shiny thin box.
                    It's stiff. My body's crying.
I try to talk it out of that physical need, but you've opened me
                                            up
already. In that other room. Took your skin off.
Let the bones just fall down.

                                    Entry 3/31/73

127

Fiction

I have been reading various fictions in a paper called *Fiction* and realize that my anger at the predictable style which repeats itself throughout its circuitous, metaphoric nature is the same as my anger towards you.

The story, as I approach it, promises to *be*, to open up something in me I don't know about. Its surface glimmers with odd and involuted phrasing which I take to be complexity— signals, symbolic but literal/as   STOP & GO & DETOUR   are on highways. But I am left with brittle paint chipping off in my hands. I reach out to touch you and your face peels.

Whatever you enjoy not showing me leaves us both as fiction—made up in this moment of what I thought was two living bodies with conscious lives reaching to touch and to open.

I feel cheated of you. I feel drawn into some deliciously painful and overextended metaphor in *your* life— that is, it's decided ahead of time. I simply serve as a new kind of food to provide energy for the fiction to continue.

A basic theme prevails, unfolds itself like a set of boxes—nothing inside as you open it but another box slightly smaller but of the exact proportions as the first, so that the boxes bear a comfortable and predictable relationship to each other.

It could be like this: you reach out, you open your voice, a stream flows out, you feel the fear fall to the sides of your face, you feel your face, you inhabit it fully, fully so that you may look beyond it. A stream of gentleness flows out. We tell each other simple things.

Entry 4/1/73